LEAN STONE PUBLISHING

"Turn the Page And Live a Better Life"

www.leanstonebookclub.com

American Civil War

Civil War: The History of America's Deadliest War - How Abraham Lincoln Ended Slavery, and the Confederate were Defeated

Table of Contents

Introduction

Today, the United States of America is one of the most powerful countries in the world. It incorporates 50 states and extends for 9.834 million km². As for its history, everybody knows the story of the Mayflower. Even though it is a much younger country than pretty much all countries in Europe, its history is nonetheless tumultuous.

The cradle of the American Dream is primarily known for the Harley bike, the Route 66, its presidents, its deep fried – everything cuisine, its implication in the 2nd World War, the Vietnam War and the Cold War. Obviously, one of the most important moments in its history, the Civil War, is known in detail by Americans, but to outsiders it's a rather obscure topic.

This Civil War that was fought for four years shaped America like no other conflict. In those that follow, we will analyze this pivotal moment in the history of the United States as we know it today, in the 21st century. We will begin with the situation in America in the 19th century, primarily in the 1860s, the election of President Abraham Lincoln and the upcoming secession crisis. Then, we will get to the conflict itself.

Let's start this historical journey through America's bloodiest war, in order for us to understand how it affected what we see and experience today.

Chapter 1 - America in 1860 and the Prelude to War

Nowadays, Abraham Lincoln is one of the most vivid personalities in American history, although he is probably more known for being assassinated by John Wilkes Booth than he is for his actual deeds. Notwithstanding, he is the most important person to focus on when talking about the situation of the United States of America in the 19th century.

One of the biggest problems in America during the 1850s and 1860s was slavery. At the time, there were roughly around 4 million slaves, mainly confined to the southern part of America. The states in the North of the country had abolished it, but the situation was entirely different in the southern states. This aspect led to the subsequent formation of two sides: the abolitionists and those who supported slavery.

Today, we do not have slavery anymore, thanks to Abraham Lincoln and his endeavors to abolish it, but back in the day, if you owned slaves, you were an accomplished person.

History has taught us that whenever there are two opposing ideologies, things can turn sour in the blink of an eye. Soon enough, there were 4 points of view, not only two. Slavery was so deeply imbibed in American everyday life that it was difficult to withdraw it, at least at a superficial level. All slaves worked as laborers. Therefore, they compiled a category of people that represented a huge workforce.

The views of the Southern Democrats and Northern Democrats differed: the former supported slavery, while the latter let the matter of whether slavery should be abolished or not in the hands of each state. The Republicans were totally against slavery, whereas the Constitutional Union Party became neutral, in the hope that the problem would clear out on its own if not given too much attention.

All these contradictory views on slavery will eventually pave the way for the outburst of many minor conflicts that, in their turn, will culminate with the Civil War. On the 27th of February 1860, Abraham Lincoln delivered his most famous speech (which, according to some historians, ensured his victory in the election): the Cooper Union Speech.

In this speech, he summoned the memory of the founding fathers in an attempt to compel those pro-slavery that it was not in the vision of those who had put the foundations of the country to have it soiled by such a horrendous act. With all these, the problem was much too serious to be solved only with a patriotic and humane appeal. Lincoln made it clear that he did not want to abolish slavery in the South. His ultimate aim was to prevent it from reaching the western part of the USA.

But, on a more positive note, the speech was incredibly effective and boosted people's trust in the soon-to-be president. This address was not very different from the one he delivered in Peoria, on the 16th of October, 1854 – he opposes slavery vehemently in both commentaries. These two speeches cement him as one of the most significant (relative) abolitionists in US history.

Before running in the election, Abraham Lincoln served as a Whig representative in the Illinois House of Representatives. This marks the moment when he becomes very steadfast about his position against the abolishment of slavery. He was also familiar with the works of John Randolph, Bushrod Washington, Charles Fenton Mercer and Herny Clay, who had been members of the American Colonization society, founded by Robert Finley in 1816. This was a group that aimed towards the emancipation of the people of color from The United

States.

Needless to say, the endeavors of the group were largely unattained. In the 1850s, he started his career as a lawyer and got the nickname of "Honest Abe." He was one of the most skilled lawyers of the time. Therefore, he was very well versed in politics, in spite of the fact that his education was quite informal. His charisma and somewhat ominous appearance inspired an unprecedented seriousness and warranted confidence more than anything else.

Another event that took place in America during the 1860s and is worth mentioning is the Paiute War, fought between the Native Americans from the Utah region, the Paiutes and the new American settlers. The first surge was fought on the 12th of May and the second between the 2nd and the 4th of June, both of them at Pyramid Lake.

As one might expect, the forces of the settlers were victorious over the few and poorly armed Paiutes. The whole thing was an overt massacre. The first battle was won by the Paiutes, but the second – and decisive – one was quickly won by the American forces.

This was not the first clash between settlers and Indians. A couple of months back, on the 26th of February, the Wiyot Massacre took place. Up to 250 Wiyot Indians were killed by the whites. They were not expecting to be attacked, since the Wiyot were known to be a peaceful tribe.

In the light of these conflicts, the US was already boiling with skirmishes. During the 1860 Republican National Convention (9th to 10th of May), Abraham Lincoln applied his candidature for becoming the 16th president of the United States. Hannibal Hamlin applied for the position of Vice President. This aspect will upset the secessionists and would kindle the little spark that would eventually set the powder keg – this is what the US was at the moment – aflame.

As we shall see next, Abraham Lincoln's victory in the election was far from being a peaceful occurrence. The signs of a bloody conflict were there for everyone to see even in the 1850s, and Lincoln was one of those who failed to see them. It did not take long until the Civil War gained momentum and exploded in proportions.

Let's take a closer look at Abraham Lincoln's presidency and how things changed in the US, unfortunately for the worst. This next section will also tackle another schismatic moment in the history of the United States: the secession.

A Series of Misconceptions about the Onset of the Civil War

The events that shaped the history of a certain country are always prone to being misunderstood. At this point, history is just a mixture of fact and myth, and those who want to discover the truth, of course, have to sieve the two. Here are a couple of things about America in the 1860s that you might think are true, but are not.

1. North America was fully anti-slavery and anti-racism

This is a half-truth. The North was more open to change than the south and it had more abolitionists, but racism was still in bloom. African Americans were lynched in North America, for instance. What came to be known as the Draft Riots also took place in the North, not the South. Therefore, North America wasn't as tolerant as you might think it was.

2. The Paiutes were obliterated instantly

Wrong. The First Battle of Pyramid Lake was won by the Paiutes. They took the whites by surprise and went all guns blazing on them. Those who surrendered, including Major Ormsby, were killed. The Indians weren't as poorly skilled in combat, nor devoid of weapons. They weren't very eager on giving their land to the settlers, which escalated in the two bloody wars within The Paiute Wars.

3. The Hall was full when Lincoln gave his Cooper Union Speech

Wrong. Even though many newspapers wrote that the room was so full of people that they couldn't find seats, it has been proven that from the almost 2,000 seats, more than a third of them were vacant.

Fascinating Facts about Abe Lincoln

Abraham Lincoln is a huge historical figure, but he was, too, a simple man with simple habits. Most of us are only familiar with his political accomplishments but don't really know much about his life. Well, let's see some fascinating – and equally outlandish – facts about him.

- Abe Lincoln was a wrestler. No, he didn't enter the ring with music in the background, nor did he wear ridiculous costumes. However, he was quite a fighter. He had around 300 matches in the ring and apparently lost only once. That's one president you wouldn't want to have messed with.

- He supported the women's right to vote. Yes, Lincoln was a feminist before it became a trend.
- He once wanted to deport African American slaves to Central America, in order to avoid the all-out conflict, i.e. the Civil War. It appears that he discussed the issue with some representatives of the minority, telling them that this move would have been beneficial for both sides (whites and African Americans).
- He suffered from depression. Lincoln's bouts of "melancholia" are no secret. Although there is no proof, he is said to have considered suicide at least two times during his life and refrained from carrying a knife, fearing that he was going to slit his own throat.

If the Choice Were Yours

- If you were Abraham Lincoln, would you have applied for presidency, knowing that you were not looked at with very good eyes by the South?
- The Wiyot Massacre was one of the most disgusting extermination programs ever because it was launched against innocent, defenseless people. If given the chance, would you condone this Massacre, even though the land on which the Wiyot people lived was never yours to take?
- How would you have dealt with the soon-to-secede states after becoming the president? Is there anything you would have done differently in order to stop the secession in its prime?

[13]

Chapter 2 - Lincoln's Election and the Secession Crisis

Abraham Lincoln was elected President of the United States on the 6th of November, 1860. He is known to have been the very first candidate of the Republican Party to win the presidential elections. However, Lincoln came into power when the United States was already on the threshold of a violent secession, and his task was a huge one.

His campaign got a lot of support from several individuals. Jesse DuBois, Norman Judd, and David Davis, among others. The Whigs, too, offered unconditional support. Given that he was against slavery, more and more people started to side with him.

Many internal problems in the US were put forth in the clear. The States were about to implode. The opinions were divided on the two most significant problems that the US was faced with: slavery and the power in the state. Never in history has been the distinction between the two parts of America, North and South, more emphasized than in the context of the pre-war period. The issue of slavery was obviously the primary cause of the secession.

The West had gotten more territories. In some circumstances, that would not have been a problem, but in these, it caused strife. Both the South and the North had bones to pick with each other on whether slavery should be encouraged or abolished in these newly-possessed territories. The South, evidently, thought that slavery should have been pushed to the new acquisitions. The North said no.

The conflict was almost palpable. But then again, there were many attempts at reaching a consensus. The Corwin

Amendment, for instance, proposed by Senator William Seward, sought to divide the lands into slavery-free and pro-slavery. As one might expect, Lincoln said he would rather die than accept the amendment.

One can easily see why Abraham Lincoln became the archenemy of many people. He wanted slavery limited to those states where it had previously existed. It was inconceivable for slavery to be employed in the territories won over in the west. Something that many people do not get is that Lincoln was not an abolitionist *per se*. It is true that he thought of it as a highly immoral thing to do, but there is another side to the story.

He did not want it abolished where it was already a thing; he just didn't want it to infiltrate to the new territories in the west. From this point of view, he is not at all a "holier-than-thou." And let us not forget that he attempted to deport the African Americans to Central America. This is somewhat of a double-edged sword. Should he have done it, maybe the Civil War could have been avoided. On the other hand, he would have ceased to be the savior people expected him to be.

What happens when you abolish slavery out of the blue? Slave-owners lose their rights, obviously. This may not seem like a tragedy to the modern reader, quite from the contrary. Owning slaves, however, was a lifestyle in the 19th century. If you owned slaves, you were similar to an aristocrat, because it meant you had money.

The South had become paranoid with the idea that Lincoln was going to deprive them of their rights, but in truth, the president had no intent whatsoever to abolish slavery there. He even made it clear in his First Inaugural address, when he said – in relation to abolishment – "[...] I have no lawful right to do so, and I have no inclination to do so."

The North always hoped that Lincoln would get rid of slavery completely, even though he never said anywhere that he would. Even though today Abraham Lincoln is seen as one of the greatest presidents of America, he was not *completely* anti-slavery, as there is enough proof to support this.

Lincoln quickly lost his status of savior and was subjected to an immense grudge. It is safe to say that he had made more enemies than friends, and as proof stand the numerous assassination attempts that ensued from November onwards. The Baltimore Plot is by far the most infamous of them all. It is debatable if an assassin was truly after Lincoln there, but the event caused a lot of hassle. Allan Pinkerton, his guard, ensured the safety of the president.

In 1861, one year after the election, 11 states had already seceded and formed the Confederate States of America. Seven states gave the start to this schism: Louisiana, Florida, South Carolina, Mississippi, Alabama, Texas, and Georgia. When the Civil War began, North Carolina, Virginia, Tennessee and Arkansas joined the Confederacy. We should mention that the "Confederacy" was, according to the North (implicitly Lincoln) illegitimate, thus a violation of the American law.

As Lincoln was cutting his teeth as president, the Confederates chose their own president (although provisional): Jefferson Davis. Davis was initially against secession, but when the states began to secede, he fully endorsed their right to do so. Even though less skilled in tactics, as well as in political prowess than Lincoln, Davis was proclaimed a hero of the South after the Civil War ended.

Later on, his wife, 18-year old Varina Davis, testified he was not happy with being chosen the president of the Confederacy. When Beauregard began the assault on Fort Sumter, Jefferson Davis endorsed the decision. Abraham Lincoln started to see that there was no backing out of the situation, and in spite of the fact that he considered the South and the North to be brothers, the break-up of the Union was not to be tolerated under any given circumstances.

A peace conference was held in the same year (1861), with the objective of reunifying the Union and the Confederation, but it was useless. If it would have had the desired effect, the Civil War would not have taken place. Seeing that the conflict reached no resolve whatsoever, Lincoln accepted going to war. However, he did not make the first step towards the conflict. He agreed that the South was to fire the first shot, so to speak.

Needless to say, it didn't take much until it did. When they attacked Fort Sumter, the entire North rallied at once under Abraham Lincoln. The anger in the air was so heavy that it was oppressive. Lincoln attempted to put down the rebellion before it escalated in the Civil War, but was unsuccessful.

Ever since he had been elected, assassins were already encircling him. And, as if he did not upset the Confederates enough, the first inaugural address he gave was replete with signs of the harsh truth that he would not abolish slavery. This was the last straw, considering that all states that had seceded were still slave-owners, but there were also many Southerners who did not agree with slavery, in any possible way.

At first, Lincoln seemed to be much of a pacifist, in the sense that he tried to reach a common ground with the Confederates and war was his last resort. Things were not as simple, however. To a certain extent, Lincoln had always been sure that the North will eventually need to battle the South, he just didn't want to give himself enough credence on this. According to many sources, the prospect of war was ghastly for him, since the South and the North had the very same blood.

It was the failed peace conference that let the president know things could not be solved with common sense. Therefore, he realized the war that had loomed its head since the '50s had to take place so that order could be established again. It has been agreed upon that the moment the Civil War began is the attack of the Confederacy on Fort Sumter, in Charleston, South Carolina. We will talk about the onset of the Civil War in the following chapter.

Top Misconceptions about the Pre-War Period

For those who are in the least familiar with history and the way it works, misconceptions are just another day at the office. Sometimes, certain facts, events, etc. are embellished to serve a purpose, although not necessarily. Let's take a look at some of the misconceptions about Lincoln's days as president and the Secession that triggered the Civil War.

1. Lincoln wanted to abolish slavery completely

You might find this redundant, considering that we've seen that Lincoln didn't want to interfere with slavery in the South, but it is still one of the grandest misconceptions concerning him and the Secession. Lincoln never said he was about to abolish slavery in the South. He just didn't want it in the new territories of the West. In this respect, he wasn't quite an abolitionist, so you might want to get your knowledge straight.

2. He wanted to send African Americans only to Central America

We have seen that he wanted to send them to Central America, but that's only one side of the story. In spite of the fact that he appeared as an abolitionist, he considered deporting the African American population back to Africa and made it public in a speech from 1894. Of course, his ideology would change, peaking with the Emancipation Proclamation. This stands to show that he had more dirt on his hands than most people

think.
3. The Union went to war to abolish slavery

That might be what you've been taught in school, but it's wrong. Abraham Lincoln decided to go to war for the sole purpose of holding the Union together. The Confederacy was a direct threat to the wholeness of the North, and this was something the president could not stand. Slavery was abolished in 1863, another argument in favor of the fact that the Union didn't get involved in the Civil War in order to give equal rights to African Americans.

Some Surprising Facts about the Secession

- Jefferson Davis voted against the secession of Mississippi. He was one of the very few who didn't see this as anything but a mistake. However, he had to comply in 1861, due to his vow of allegiance. But again, he was not a secessionist, as ironic as it may seem.
- Lincoln was the first Republican president in the history of the United States. Moreover, he was the first president that was not born in the first 13 colonies; he was the tallest of all US presidents and the first leader to be branded on a coin.
- Lincoln was nicknamed the "Rail Candidate" because he used to split rails with his father.

If the Choice Were Yours

- If you were Abraham Lincoln, would you have started the Civil War, as in attack the South, or would you have waited for the Confederacy to attack first, as the president did?

- The Corwin Amendment could have potentially avoided the start of a bloody conflict, but slavery would have still existed. Would you have accepted the terms outlined in the document, or would you have chided it, as Lincoln did?
- If given a chance, what would you do to stop the war from escalating in a nationwide one? Would you try to continue to reason or would you go all guns blazing?

Chapter 3 - The Mobilization & the Western and Eastern Theatres

On the 12th of April 1861, the Confederate Army opened fire on Fort Sumter. This was so much more than a simple bombardment: it struck the match on the upcoming Civil War. The Fort was extremely under prepared for a siege. The Confederacy took advantage of that. It is known that Abraham Lincoln was well-aware of the poor condition of the Fort and had planned to send another fleet there.

The Confederate forces were quicker, however. Pierre Beauregard, the Confederate General, asked Anderson to surrender. He refused for the second time, so Beauregard ordered to open the fire on the fort. The Union resisted the bombardment for well over 24 hours before all the people in the fort surrendered. There were no casualties whatsoever.

There were reports of a shell going off and killing two soldiers with allegiance to the Union, but there were no other casualties *per se*. If Anderson would not have surrendered the fort, Beauregard, with 6,000 men under his command, would have transformed Fort Sumter in a pile of debris and ash, in spite of the fact that the Confederates had ammunition to assault the Fort for just two days.

The following aspect marks the unfolding of the bloody massacre. Whereas the artillery bombardment of the fort did not claim any life at all, the remainder will. As quickly as the meager forces of the Union were evacuated out of Fort Sumter, Abraham Lincoln deployed 75.000 volunteers to rush there and quench the mutiny.

This started the war and also made four more states to secede: North Carolina, Virginia, Arkansas and Tennessee. Therefore, the Confederacy became an even bigger threat to the integrity

[21]

of the Union. Abraham Lincoln soon found out that some Northern states were not willing to send troops to fight the Southern ones. Missouri and Kentucky refused to answer the call to arms. Ohio, on the other hand, amassed the 75,000 volunteers asked for by Lincoln on its own.

Even nowadays, in the 21st century, it is hard to fathom the reason why a few millions of Americans were willing to indulge in this 4-year bloodshed. Anyhow, the number of the Confederate forces multiplied as quickly as the number of the Union troops. The Union got many people from the ranks of immigrants and even former slaves on its side. That is not surprising at all.

With all these, the African Americans who served in the Union Army refused to take their salary for 18 months, starting with 1862. That didn't happen because they were just happy to fight for their freedom, but because they were paid less than the White Union soldiers, almost half of what they got. They got equal pay only after two years.

To give you a hint of the big picture here, the African Americans were charged even for the clothes they were wearing in battle. The tax was 3 dollars which were, of course, taken from their pay. This further enhanced their outrage, although they did not desert.

At first, neither Lincoln nor Davis expected this war to last for so long. Raising people to fight by their side was not a task as easy as they thought it would be. First of all, Southerners *hoped* the conflict wouldn't last because, in the long run, the North was still more powerful. The industry was a lot better. Therefore, the North could come with virtually endless supplies of weapons and bullets, whereas the South had very few resources for manufacturing guns.

There are many other factors that applied to the North but

failed to apply to the South. For instance, the South was mainly agrarian, while the North was industrialized (not *that* much, but still). And of course, the Union had better demographics and did not rely on slaves.

There have been countless theories that the South could have won if it would have done this and that, but for each such theory, a double number of historians are quick in relinquishing it. One historian went as far as to say that in the Civil War, the North fought at 50% capability. If it would've given 100%, the war would have lasted less than a half of the four year-period.

The Theaters

There were two theaters within the Civil War: the Eastern one and the Western one. The former encompassed West Virginia, Virginia, Pennsylvania, coastal North Carolina and Washington DC. The latter was primarily comprised of Florida, Carolina and the stretch of terrain from the Allegheny Mountains to Mississippi. A third intermediate theater, the Trans-Mississippi, was established in the western part of the Mississippi River, including Arkansas, Texas, Oklahoma, Missouri and lastly, Louisiana.

The start of the long chain of battles was given in Philippi, where a considerable number of Union forces descended upon a weak formation of Confederates. Most historians agree on the fact that this does not qualify as a fight since it did not take more than 30 minutes. The next one, however, has everything a battle needs to be worthy of its denomination.

On the 21st of July, 1861, the first true battle occurred: the First Battle of Bull Run. This took place in the proximity of Manassas, Virginia. The forces of the Confederacy were led by Joseph E. Johnston, P.G.T. Beauregard, Thomas Jackson and the ones of the Union by Winfield Scott, Irvin McDowell and Robert Patterson.

Even though both sides had relatively equal forces engaged in combat, the Union had to retreat. Initially, Irvin McDowell had the upper hand because he had launched a surprise attack on the Confederates. Anyway, the soldiers of the Union were so poorly skilled that they couldn't pull the attack off and the Confederates woke up from the surprise almost immediately. The generals of the Union were poorly skilled in warfare, and they did not manage to engage the full bulk of forces. The first battle in the context of the Civil War was won by the Confederates.

Johnston's forces got to the site of the battle quickly, and the Union was forced to retreat, suffering almost 3,000 casualties in the process. This first battle was marred by pathetic strategies that encompassed everything that can be deemed "diving headfirst" and the fact that most of the soldiers were only partially committed to the ideals of the armies they belonged to.

Needless to say, Lincoln was baffled by the monumental defeat of his Union army. All northerners expected the Union to have an easy victory against the Confederacy at Bull Run. Just like he did before when the Confederates employed battery on the Fort, he called forth hundreds of thousands of volunteers. This happened on the 22nd of July. Three days later, the Pennsylvania Reserves, as they were later called, came into being.

Pennsylvanians mainly fought in the Eastern Theater, where they suffered massive casualties due to being severely inexperienced in battle. The fact that the same soldiers had been rejected initially by Lincoln stands to show he was now going to an all-out war and was willing to make a lot of compromises. After Bull Run, Davis supplemented the forces of the Confederacy, as well. This is a very important moment. Thus, we have to treat it accordingly: when the Pennsylvania Reserves were summoned by Lincoln, this was a sign of alarm.

What did it mean? It's simple and as horrifying as it is simple: the Civil War was not going to be this short-lived conflict that would quench itself in a couple of months. It was going to take a while. Neither Lincoln nor Davis would have hoped that it will take no less than 4 years until this skirmish will eventually die out. The Battle of Bull Run, although short-lived, was massive. Were it not so, the leaders would have known that it would have been the single battle between the South and the North. However, the viciousness showcased during the conflict was tell-tale.

In the following months, the Union was defeated on multiple occasions by the Confederacy. The Battle of Oak Hills, for instance, is one of them. This time, the Union forces were under the leadership of Nathaniel Lyon, Franz Sigel, and Samuel Sturgis, whereas the ones of the Confederates were led by Sterling Price, Nicholas Pearce, and Ben McCulloch. Lyon attacked first, managing to push the Confederates off the Bloody Hill, but the Confederates soon responded with three attacks that eventually made the Union, once again, retreat.

The streak of severe Union defeats does not stop here. Tens of battles were fought in the Eastern and Western theaters, as well as in the so-called Trans-Mississippi Theater. The Union somehow managed to win some battles, too: Battle of Boonville, Hoke's Run, Rich Mountain, Hatteras Inlet, Carnifex Ferry, Cheat Mountain, etc.

In 1862, the Second Battle of Bull Run occurred. This was one of the most catastrophic events for the Union, as it had to retreat again, faced with utter destruction. However, 1862 proved to be a good year for the North, as it gained some of its morale back. Whereas in the previous year, most battles were won by the Confederacy, the tables turned a year later. We could never tackle all the conflicts in just one take, not even those in a single year.

The Union eventually got an immense boost, both in forces and encouragement in 1863. By contrast, the Confederacy found itself in quite a pickle. This is one of the key moments in the Civil War:

The Emancipation Proclamation

On January 1st, 1863, Abraham Lincoln took Southerners by storm by issuing the Emancipation Proclamation. This document stated that all African-American people who had been enslaved in Southern states were suddenly given freedom. Their numbers were in the millions. Out of the blue, all slaves were now free.

Maybe it's a little far-fetched to say they were "free": socially, the Proclamation didn't change the status of the African Americans that much, especially in the South, where the enraged slave owners pled for death for those slaves who left. However, Lincoln knew the advantages of the document when he issued it.

This will prove to be a stroke of genius. Why? Because it turned the tides of war in favor of the Union. The South had won so many battles because the aforementioned slaves had been used as help in the war. They cooked for the Southerners, they sewed their clothes, and they provided medical care and all in all, looked for their masters. They were not allowed to enlist in the Confederate army, but they labored day and night for it, anyway. When they were given another alternative, i.e. run from their masters and join the ranks of the Union Army, they didn't wait too much to do it.

When the Emancipation Proclamation ensued, the Confederacy realized it had lost one of its most important assets in the war against the Union. Former slaves now fled and joined the Union forces. Lincoln was immediately embraced by the North. The African-American population now had the chance to take vengeance on the South that had allowed for them to be treated poorly. The forces of the Union grew virtually in a blink of an eye, much to the chagrin of the Confederates.

And not only this: Europe was very pleased to see that Abraham Lincoln had finally taken the final step in abolishing slavery. The Union was, therefore, a lot more favored than the Confederacy. Bad news for the latter, again. The Confederacy wished for international recognition, too, but this time the Union was a lot quicker.

We must mention another crucial aspect regarding this proclamation: it had effect only on those mutinous states in the Confederacy. Therefore, it is like Lincoln sucker punched the South. Not only was the North growing more confident and powerful, but the African-American people now had an unquenchable drive to fight abreast the Union with a personal objective in mind: their own liberation.

Many people think that the Emancipation Proclamation made slavery illicit, but it wasn't so. Slavery wasn't outlawed. Moreover, 1 million African American people were still slaves, because the Proclamation was in effect only in certain states. The neutral states were not affected by it. Therefore, the African American population in them had the exact same status of slaves.

On the 22nd of September, 1862, Abraham Lincoln attempted to put an end to the war by threatening the states that were still attacking the Union forces that he will issue a national emancipation. In other words, this new document would have ended slavery in all states, regardless of which those were. As one might expect, none of the Confederate states was eager to stop the rebelliousness. The total emancipation proclamation from January 1st, 1863 was therefore ensued.

After the Emancipation Proclamation, two of the bloodiest and most important battles of the Civil War took place: one at Vicksburg and the other one at Gettysburg. The former was fought between the 18th of May and the 4th of July, while the latter between 1-3 July. These two battles changed the course of the war completely.

The Battle of Vicksburg

The Battle of Vicksburg or the Siege of Vicksburg, as it is also known, was the first major, decisive Union victory over the Confederacy. With a fresh morale and forces, the Union made an unbelievable comeback. Vicksburg was one of the last Confederate garrisons on Mississippi.

Ulysses S. Grant was in charge of the USA army, while John C. Pemberton was in charge of the Confederate army, the Army of Mississippi, to be more precise. The CSA had 30,000 soldiers. The Union a little over 70,000, therefore more than double the force of the Confederacy.

The Union had attempted to conquer Vicksburg in 1862, too, but a lack of land troops made it impossible. Why was Vicksburg so important for the Union? Because it served a grander purpose: the Anaconda Plan (which implied smothering the ports of the South) needed this fortress to work properly.

Initially, the Union suffered heavy casualties. It was obvious that a wave of attacks would not be effective against the Confederacy because the defenses were pretty solid.

[28]

The first wave of the assault ordered by Grant was not very efficient. The second assault again, cost the Union lives, as the forces were not able to penetrate through the Confederate defense, even though artillery had weakened it to some extent. Somewhere around a total of 6-7 attacks were repulsed by the Confederates. Needless to say, Grant was enraged.

A total siege was warranted. Under continuous artillery fire, the Confederates were forced to either surrender or face their utter destruction. The Union bombarded the fort day and night, without stopping. Some of the siege waves were repelled by the Confederacy, but the forces of the Union were too many, so the Confederates had to surrender. The Union, at some point, blew up an entire mine so that they could rip the Confederate defense lines apart, leaving them in the open, with nothing to serve as protection.

A mistake has been made, however: Ulysses S. Grant, the general in charge with the siege of Vicksburg paroled all soldiers after they surrendered unconditionally. In the short run, this was a good idea, because it cut the costs the Union would have had to spend to feed them all while in prison. In the long run, most of these paroled soldiers returned in the army of the Confederacy in the following months. Maybe the fact that Grant got tens of thousands of rifles and over 150 Confederate cannons was worth the liberation of the Confederacy soldiers.

In the Battle of Vicksburg, somewhere around 3,000 Confederate soldiers lost their lives and were wounded. The casualties were greater for the Union: 4,000 killed and wounded, due to wrong moves on the onset of the battle, when Grant ordered for an all-out siege, underestimating the defensive forces of the Confederates waiting in the fortress.

The Battle of Gettysburg

The Battle of Gettysburg is one of the shortest but simultaneously bloodiest conflicts in the Civil War. Moreover, it provided a jab of hope to the North that somehow ensured that the Confederacy was already headed towards its last days. At first, Confederates didn't see this loss as much of a tragedy, but then it became quite obvious that the battle meant so much more for both sides, in particular for the Union.

In this battle, tens of thousands of soldiers perished. The Confederacy lost somewhere around 28,000 people, while the Union lost 23,000 or so. This clash between the Army of the Potomac (Union), under the command of George G. Meade and the Army of Northern Virginia (Confederacy), led by Robert E. Lee took two days, but it claimed more lives than weeks of war. This battle also featured the renowned general, Robert E. Lee, who will surrender his army over to Ulysses Grant and put an end to the Civil War in 1865.

The Battle of Gettysburg began on the 1st of July, 1863, and ended on the 3rd of the same month. During the first day of battle, the Confederate forces were able to break through the Union's defense lines. The assaults of both armies were huge, almost apocalyptical because, on the second day, the entire bulks of the Union and the Confederacy clashed in one another. Cemetery Hill, Culp's Hill, the Peach Orchard and Cemetery Ridge were the locations where most of the bloodshed happened.

Despite massive assaults from the Confederates, the Union divisions were steadfast in standing their ground, which resulted in incredibly high casualties for both sides. On the third day, Lee, bored already with the determination of the Union soldiers who stood in his way to conquering the North, sent a little over 12,000 soldiers straight into the defensive position of the Union. Thanks to being in a strategic place, the Union soldiers disintegrated Lee's army with a combination of infernal artillery and rifle showers.

Lee, seeing that he was about to lose the battle, called the Confederate army to retreat back to Virginia. As they were retreating, the Union launched another attack on the Confederates, thinning their numbers once more. A total of 11 battles took place during the retreat from Gettysburg, as the Union continued to harass the weak Confederate army. In the previous battles, it was almost always the Confederate initiating the attacks. The Battle of Gettysburg, therefore, was a turning point. The predator became the prey, so to speak.

The Union continued to harass the scant forces of the Confederacy, constantly pushing back its army towards Virginia or attacking it with no prior announcement, dealing huge damage.

4 months after the Battle of Gettysburg was fought, Abraham Lincoln delivered his famous Gettysburg speech, on the 19th of November, 1863. He once again made statements about equality and interconnected the losses of lives in the eponymous battle as a much-needed sacrifice for a newly-born Union. Evidently, he expressed his sadness towards the bloodshed that had taken place. One of the most interesting things concerning his Gettysburg Address is that he spoke for approximately 10 minutes, but his speech went down in history books.

Edward Everett, a so-called "orator", also talked at the Soldiers' National Cemetery. He talked about Gettysburg for around 2 hours and didn't say much, even though it took him so long to finish his speech. This stands to show that when Abraham Lincoln opened his mouth, history listened very carefully. Unfortunately, his speech has not been preserved for future generations to read. Even though the speech was an optimistic one, two more years would pass until the Civil War would come to an end.

1864 debuted with the victory of the Confederates at the Battle of Dandridge (17th of January) and followed, like in the previous years, with a multitude of both minor and major battles. However, the Union was growing increasingly powerful, and the signs that the Confederacy was going to perish eventually were all the more visible.

Starting with 1865, the Union begins to win battle after battle, much to the chagrin of the weakened Southerners. The Union had five consecutive victories: the Second Battle of Fort Fisher (14-15 January), Battle of River's Bridge (3rd of February), Battle of Hatcher's Run (5-7 February), Battle of Wilmington (22nd of February) and Battle of Waynesboro (2nd of March).

Obviously, battles were not fought only on soil, but on waters, too. Let's take a look at the naval wars in the Civil War, for they are as fascinating as the ones that have been fought on land.

Misconceptions about the Civil War

The Civil War is not devoid of misconceptions. Quite from the contrary. Most people are not able to distinguish between fact and fiction when they discuss about this conflict. Because of that, we took the liberty of busting a few of the greatest myths about the Civil War that you might have taken as truth.

1. **The Confederate ranks were joined by the slaves**

Wrong. The Confederacy did not allow African Americans to fight with the whites until 1865, when the war was drawing to an end, anyway. Of course, the situation in the Union was entirely different. The North indeed got help from many regiments of African American people. When Jefferson Davis was presented the idea that the slaves could come in handy in the theaters, he rebuked it immediately. In 1865, however, when the Confederacy was one step away from being destroyed, he allowed slaves to enlist in the army.

2. Soldiers in the Civil War were not butchered by surgeons

This is without a doubt one of the greatest misconceptions about the Civil War ever. A lot of people glorify the soldiers who apparently used alcohol to numb themselves, albeit rather inefficiently, before the surgeon cut them open. That was simply not the case. The surgeons had anesthesia, even though it was not as modern as it is today. They used chloroform. Antibiotics did not exist back in those days, and that is why limbs had to be taken off. Soldiers had more chances of surviving the surgeries than they had chances of surviving infected wounds.

3. With better strategy, the South could have won the Civil War

Nope. It couldn't. In the end, all wars boil down to the numbers. The side with the higher numbers always wins. The Confederacy was doomed to fail even before the Civil War broke out, simply because it didn't have sufficient manpower to withstand the forces of the Union, let alone win against them.

Some of the Most Spellbinding Facts about the Civil War

Apart from misconceptions, history offers us some of the funniest and most fascinating things about the period we are studying. Here are some of the most mind-blowing facts you definitely had no idea about.

- During the Civil War, many soldiers reported that some of the wounds glowed in the dark. And no, it wasn't their imagination: some really did glow, thanks to a bacterium called *Photorhabdus luminescens*. It appeared that the soldiers whose wounds were glowing recovered at a much faster pace than the ones whose wounds did not glow. This bacterium actually produced antibiotics in the wounds of the soldiers who suffered of hypothermia (the bacteria cannot survive the normal heat of the human body) and glowed in the process.
- Martin Greene, a Confederate general, boasted that "A bullet has not yet been molded that will kill me." He was shot in the head a few seconds later.
- Walt Whitman, one of the most praised poets in American literature, served in the Civil War. He was a nurse.
- In 1863, Abraham Lincoln was almost assassinated. Somebody shot at him. When he retrieved his hat, which he thought simply fell off his head, he observed a bullet hole in it.

If the Choice Were Yours

- If given the chance, would you order the attack on Fort Sumter, well-knowing that this would ignite a nationwide war that would claim hundreds of thousands of lives?
- The Emancipation Proclamation was a very low blow given by Abraham Lincoln to the Confederacy. It is the definition of "sucker-punch." If you were him, would you have ensued the Proclamation as a military tool,

like he did, or out of humanitarian feeling, in order to emancipate the African-American population, who had been enslaved for so long?

- Ulysses Grant allowed the Confederacy soldiers to go unharmed after they surrendered at Vicksburg. We've seen that they just went back to the Confederate Army. Would you have done the same mistake?

Chapter 4 - The Naval Wars

Ever since the onset of the Civil War, supremacy on water was one of the main objectives of both the Union and the Confederacy. The Anaconda Plan, for instance, is perhaps the most known appanage of the Union in this respect. This consisted of a large-scale blockade of the main ports in the South. It was not effective until two years later.

This blockade was supposed to reduce the amount of bloodshed that would have been otherwise needed in 1861 to suppress the rising forces of the Confederacy. However, plans like these seldom work as outlined. First of all, when you block ports, you need a huge number of forces to ensure that the ports remain in the influence of the Union. This was not the case then.

The Union was superior to the Confederacy in terms of naval prowess. Moreover, the Union had cut off its cotton trade, an aspect which destabilized the economy of the South, albeit not permanently. Advised by highly competent assistants, Abraham Lincoln was able to boost the maritime power to such an extent that it almost looks surreal.

In 1861, the Union did not have more than 90 warships. In a short period, it had over 600 and more than 55,000 sailors. The Confederacy had very few. Southerners had to purchase and build warships, as well as restore old ones to match the power of the Union. When talking about naval wars in the context of the Civil War, we are not looking at a moment of simple on-water conflict.

The 19th century saw myriad innovations in terms of warfare, most notably the use of submarines and armored warships (ironclads). Ironclads were ships defended by steel plates, virtually indestructible unless the fire was focused on weak points. These prototypes quickly replaced the already old steam-powered ships, that were both weak in terms of maximum speed (ironclads were not that fast either) and building materials.

The naval conflicts obviously began in 1861, with the siege of Fort Sumter. The most important stages in the naval skirmish between the Union and the Confederacy are as follows: the Battle of Hampton Roads, the First Battle of Charleston Harbor and finally, the Battle of Cherbourg. Of course, we mustn't forget about the Battle of Port Royal, one of the first major victories of the Union, which took place between the 3rd and the 7th of November, 1861. In this battle, the fleet of the Union got ahold of the Port Royal, in South Carolina.

Let's take a closer look at each of the battles above, in order to see who won and what each victory or loss meant for the sides that were subjected to them.

The Battle of Hampton Roads (8-9 March, 1862)

Often deemed as the most significant on-water battle in the Civil War, this saw the use of ironclad warships. The Union had the USS Monitor, whereas the Confederacy had the CSS Virginia. On the first day of battle, the Union sent a few poor, wooden ships to withstand the CSS Virginia. Huge mistake.

Needless to say, *Virginia* ripped them to shreds. The first Union ship to go under was the Cumberland, which did not last long on water. *Congress* followed. This was an incredible victory for the Confederacy, and it is safe to say that nobody would have expected the South to be able to inflict so much damage on the ships of the Union.

When the USS Monitor joined the battle, it was obvious that

both ships were equal in terms of power and defense. They shot at each other for hours, but none of them could do lethal damage to the other. However, John L. Worden, the commander of the USS Monitor was blinded by shrapnel of iron from a shell launched from the Confederate Virginia. Samuel Dana Green took the command and returned to the site of the battle.

The Monitor retreated and so did the CSS Virginia. The latter was in desperate need of reparations. When Green saw the departing Virginia, he thought that the Confederates had given up on fighting. The Confederates, on the other hand, were certain they had won the battle because the Monitor had left the waters. It is still debatable which side won this naval battle. One thing is certain: both sides claimed the victory.

The Confederates were praised by Stephen Mallory, the Secretary of the Navy. The Union was praised, too, by the Congress, when, in reality, none of the sides had really won the conflict. It is one of the many hilarious instances during the Civil War.

Considering the massive damage done by Virginia on the Union fleet, we are inclined to believe that it was the Confederacy that won it. This naval battle is extremely important because it stands to show that the Confederacy, although in an obvious inferiority of number of forces was more than capable of doing considerable damage to the Union.

The Confederate Virginia was eventually destroyed by the Confederates themselves because it had gotten stuck in the James River. The Union's Monitor, too, was destroyed, while heading towards North Carolina. It was caught in a storm, caught water and sank in 1862, on the 31st of December, drowning 16 sailors.

The Monitor was recovered in a maritime expedition in 1973.

The wreck was found at the bottom of the ocean, where it stood for more than a century. Several original items found on the wreck are displayed in the Mariners' Museum in Virginia.

The First Battle of Charleston Harbor (7th of April, 1863)

As we've seen until now, the Union underestimated the naval power of the South. Severely. In the Battle of Charleston Harbor, the Confederacy proved that it wasn't as helpless as it was thought to be. Whereas the North had two ironclad warships engaged in battle, plus seven monitors, the South had two ironclads, as well, assisted by almost 400 guns firing from the shores. The Confederate ships were commanded by P.G.T. Beauregard, whereas the ones of the Union were under the leadership of Samuel Francis Du Pont.

Even though the Union had a lot more ships, the Confederacy was able to repel quite easily. This battle ended with a resounding victory for the South, in spite of the superiority of the North. On the next day, 8th of April, the USS Keokuk, an ironclad commissioned for the Union was sunk. It had taken so much gunfire that it could not be repaired under any circumstances.

The battle lasted only one day because Du Pont refused to return to the harbor, well-knowing he had no chance of beating the Confederate forces into submission, even more so that they were firing severely from the shores. Even though it looks like a very bloody battle, it really was not. The Confederates lost five men and had eight wounded, while the Union lost 1 and had 21 wounded, plus a sunken ship.

The Union did not take Du Pont's withdrawal all that good. Because so few were wounded, the Secretary of the Navy initially thought the commander had not been sufficiently determined. Du Pont tried to defend himself by saying that he was all-in for going to battle again the next morning, but all his captains had vetoed. Even when Du Pont's claims were supported by John Rodgers, an extremely capable officer, Du Pont was ultimately replaced with Andrew Foote, and then with John A. Dahlgren.

This was quite a sad loss for the Union because the Keokuk seemed indestructible. The South proved otherwise. Story has it that more than 90 projectiles hit the ironclad. It did not go easy, but it was sunk eventually because it took too many hits under the waterline. As quickly as it was sunk, the Confederates did not miss the chance of retrieving the Dahlgren guns that went to the bottom with it.

They did not possess such incredible weapons, so it is easy to understand why a salvage operation began immediately. They did indeed retrieve the guns and used them until the War ended. Chicora and Palmetto State were two ironclads used by the Confederates when they retrieved the weapons. If the forces of the Union would have been notified on their mission, they would have needed protection. Fortunately for them, the Union had no idea whatsoever that the Confederacy was stealing from the Keokuk. They found out much later after the guns were already gone.

The Battle of Cherbourg (19th of June, 1864)

Now we finally move on to a naval victory of the Union. The main warships engaged in combat were the USS Kearsarge (Union) and the CSS Alabama (Confederacy). The commanders were John Winslow (the Union) and Raphael Semmes (the Confederacy). CSS Alabama was a really feared ship. It dealt great damage to the Union, especially against its merchant ships, during its commerce raiding sessions.

Commerce raiding was a popular tactic in the 19th century, and before it. A weaker naval army cannot compete with a larger one overtly. The same thing applies for warfare on land. What can it do in this case?

Simple: it captures and destroys its merchant ships so that the enemy loses money and valuable goods like food and supplies. It is especially helpful as a harassing tactic. This is precisely what the CSS Alabama was doing. It dared the waters, captured Union merchant ships and looted them, eventually sinking the ships. This would not have been such a disaster, but the Union was in need of certain products. Needless to say, it didn't get them.

The two ships had pursued each other for approximately two years until they met in French waters. The victory of the Kearsarge can be explained by the technology it was endowed with. To tell the whole truth, the USS Kearsarge was a testing/experimental warship. The guns on it fired at a much slower rate than those on the CSS Alabama.

However, when shots are fired at a slower rate, they are automatically more accurate. The chaotic firing of the CSS Alabama did not have much success. This could have been great against wooden, steam-driven ships, but not against an ironclad. Eventually, shots were fired by the Kearsarge under the waterline and made holes in the Alabama. Heavy fire continued and the Confederate warship sunk.

In spite of the fact that Alabama fired almost 400 rounds, it had no chance, really, against the USS Kearsarge. The number of rounds fired from this ship is unknown, but it could be as low as half the number of those fired from the CSS Alabama. Meanwhile, the exquisite "spectacle" was watched by hundreds of people off the coast of Cherbourg. It was a free show for them.

The Battle of Cherbourg was followed by the deadly, vicious Battle of Mobile Bay (August 5), in which the Union had a huge victory. The Confederate CSS Tennessee was sunk and around 1,500 Confederates were taken prisoners. This was one of the Union's easiest naval victories thanks to the number of its forces. In previous occasions, the number didn't actually offer much help to the Union, but now the heavens had opened its eyes on it, for the first time in a while.

It has been claimed that the Union had around 5,000+ men, whereas the Confederation only had 1,500. This victory came very handy for Abraham Lincoln, who once again ran for president in November, the same year. It was used as some kind of leverage that rose him in people's eyes. Lincoln did win his second run to the presidency but unfortunately passed away early on during his second term, leaving the same Johnson that delivered an intoxicated speech at his inauguration at the wheel.

At this point, it certainly looks like the Confederacy began to dominate the Union both on land and on waters initially, but then completely lost its drive. 51 naval battles were fought between the two forces during the Civil War. Surely, all ships contributed to the results of the battles led on land, as well, because they were used for transportation of goods, guns, and soldiers.

Everything pointed towards the ruination of the Confederacy, a moment that we will further analyze in the following chapters. We shall also see what this meant for the "melting pot" of today.

A List of Misconceptions about the Civil War Naval Battles

1. The South couldn't match the naval power of the North

Wrong. Initially, yes, the South was extremely disadvantaged, because it had to either buy or build ships, while the North already had them. That, however, was not really a problem for the Confederacy. In a very short period, it was able not only to match the Union in terms of military power on the waters but to undermine it. The vast majority of the naval battles in the Civil War were won by the Confederacy because their strategies were considerably better than the North's.

2. Cutting down the cotton trade of the South was the only thing that led to economic trouble

Again, wrong. There has been proof that the North actually counterfeited Confederacy bills in order to start the inflation. The cotton trade, of course, brought some more money to the South and definitely contributed to the weak economy there, but it was just the tip of the iceberg.

3. The Anaconda plan worked like a charm

Half-true. It did work for the Union but after a while. In 1861, almost all Confederate ships were able to break through the blockade. At first, most people were not eager on accepting the plan. Would they have done so, the Civil War could have potentially ended in just a few weeks. Unfortunately, it wasn't as useful in practice as it was in theory. It will be close to the end of the Civil War that the Anaconda Plan – or better said, what had remained of Scott's original plan – would be implemented.

[43]

Fascinating Facts about the Naval Battles

- The USS Housatonic was the first ship to be sunken by a submarine. The submarine that did it was called H. L. Hunley and belonged to the Confederacy.
- The USS Kearsarge that fought during the Civil War has been commemorated by other ships that borrowed its name. The USS Kearsarge LHD-3, for instance, is one of those. The LHD-3 is active, and it was launched in 1992, on the 26th of March.
- Four American ships were named after the late Union Navy Officer, John Lorimer Worden: Worden DD-16 (destroyer), Worden DD-288 (destroyer), Worden DD-352 (destroyer) and Worden CG-18 (cruiser).

If the Choice Were Yours

- General Winfield Scott, the creator of the Anaconda Plan, was ridiculed for this strategy that could have saved thousands of lives, if not avoid the Civil War entirely. Would you have pushed the idea forward, or would you have resigned believing in it yourself? Keep in mind that the North eventually saw that its victory could have been achieved a lot quicker if Scott had been given the credit he deserved.
- In The Battle of Hampton Roads, the Union tried to withstand the ironclad CSS Virginia with a few wooden ships. Would you have done the same if you had the chance or not, considering that you could have spared some lives from absolute destruction?
- The CSS Alabama was in some severe trouble in fighting against the USS Kearsarge. Would you have continued the fight, seeing that the Kearsarge inflicted

incredible damage on the ship, or would you have left the waters in order to avoid being sunken?

Chapter 5 - Conquest of Virginia & the Confederate Surrender

Starting from 1864, it was clear that the days of the Confederacy were numbered. Virginia, the first state that had seceded from the Union was to be the last one to be reduced to ashes. Eight battles were fought there in the final year of the war: at Namozine Church, at Amelia Springs, Rice's Station, Sayler's Creek, High Bridge, Cumberland Church, The Third Battle of Petersburg, Appomattox Station and Appomattox Court House.

The Union won most of these. One that bears interest to us is the one that took place in Petersburg, Virginia, the precursor to the conflicts unleashed in Appomattox. Once again, Ulysses Grant and Robert Lee were in charge of their armies, the Union's and the Confederacy's respectively.

In this battle, fought on the 2nd of April, 1865, the forces of the Confederacy were extremely thin. Grant had charged through the rows more than once, killing and wounding Confederate soldiers left and right. One day later, the army of the Union got in Richmond and Petersburg. Most of the Confederates caught in the middle had to either flee or be killed.

Even though Lee's army had retreated, the Union, thanks to a considerably superior number of soldiers, managed to encircle the rebels. This led to the Confederate surrender on April 9th, 1865. The forces of the Confederacy had been smashed across the state of Virginia, and they had no food. The Battle of Appomattox Court House was the decisive one, although this was the penultimate battle in the Civil War, not the last one. Abraham Lincoln had appointed the highly skilled and very efficient Ulysses S. Grant to wreak havoc in Virginia.

If we take a look at the numbers involved in this battle, it should not come as a surprise at all that the Union won without too much hassle. In the Battle of Appomattox Court House, the Union had a strength of 150,000, whereas the Confederacy had a little over 27,500. The Confederate army was led by Robert E. Lee, a capable general and one of Jefferson Davis' most influential advisers in terms of warfare and military tactics, but charging against the Union forces was very much of a fiasco, as it would have been just like sending sheep to the slaughterhouse.

Why is this battle so important? Because it marks the moment when the Confederacy trembles from the foundations and crumbles under its own weight. It was fought on April 9, 1865. On the eve of the battle, the Union did not spare the Confederacy at all. Grant engaged the bulk of the army to go with full force against the Confederate army, as a last attempt to conquer Virginia and to end the Civil War.

Needless to say, he did not need to go berserk on the forces of the Confederacy because: 1) they were extremely meager and 2) they were starving and therefore had no energy left for fighting effectively.

Petersburg and Richmond had been ransacked by Grant's army, so the provisions of the Confederate soldiers were almost inexistent. After the battle of High Bridge, Grant attempted to make Lee surrender, but the general was not willing to do that just yet. With all these, he showed interest in the terms of the surrender.

Perhaps the thought of surrendering was not as dismal as he gave the impression it was. He would not have surrendered if the number of the Union forces were a little smaller, but in this case, he quickly found that he was dealing with something he could not win against, by any means.

Outcomes of the Battle of Appomattox Court House

Around 500 Confederate soldiers were killed before Robert E. Lee realized he could not withstand such an enormous army. The Union lost approximately 160 people. Lee was advised by his peers that they only had one solution left to avoid utter slaughter: surrender. Lee had been a brilliant general who saved his soldiers more than once, while simultaneously stopping Grant's assaults. This time, however, he was bound to fail and to finally see his Confederate army being stopped from delivering severe blows to the Union.

At first, Lee did not like the prospect of surrendering, but this can be attributed to wounded pride more than anything else. He is reported to have said that he would have rather died uncountable times than give in to Grant. Even so, he had no other possible choice. For us nowadays, it's easy to say that he could have fought until the end. Fighting is one thing, but going straight to the massacre is an entirely different thing.

He eventually sent Ulysses Grant a letter in which he requested to meet him. The Union general accepted, and the two leaders met at the McLean House (which can be visited even today, albeit it is a reconstruction). Of course, a ceasefire was installed while Grant and Lee exchanged correspondence. When they met, Grant offered Lee extremely generous terms for the surrender of his army: the Confederate soldiers had to vow they were not going to pick arms against the Union again and all guns had to be surrendered over to the generals of the Union, as well.

The officers were allowed to keep their weapons, however, and their private possessions as well. What made Lee breathe again with renewed hope was Grant's clause that all the Confederate soldiers were free to return to their homes without any strings attached. That is, they did not face a lifetime in prison nor prosecution in the courthouse.

The Civil War had ended finally. The fact that the soldiers were not going to be prosecuted inspired other Confederates to lie their weapons down. The cause was lost, and there was obviously no reason why they should have stuck to them.

It meant that the Union was kind of right: Southerners and Northerners were indeed brothers and sisters, and there was no reason for waging war against one another again. It took them 4 years to realize that, but it's better late than never. The period after the surrender of the Army of Northern Virginia is marked by a cessation of conflict (although small skirmishes were still condoned in the theaters) and a quick installation of the restoration.

All the soldiers of the Confederacy stacked their guns and left. Lee's surrender was followed by a surge of other Confederate surrenders. Joseph Johnston surrendered on the 26th of April, Nathan Bedford on the 9th of May, Richard Taylor on the 26th of May, Stand Watie on the 23rd of June.

While more than 90% of the people are inclined to think that the Civil War ended immediately when Lee signed the surrender papers, it did not. 23rd of June is the real date on which the War ended, because minor clashes between the Union and the Confederacy still happened until then. Some researchers went as far as to say that on waters, the Civil War continued until November of the same year.

Lee, as stipulated in the terms of the surrender, was not arrested. He continued to be active in politics. He supported the idea of equal rights for everybody, but he was not in favor of granting the black population the right to vote. He became the president of nowadays Washington and Lee University from Virginia.

Apparently, Lee became a father figure for the students. All of them loved him because he commanded a certain respect and was always interested in whether all students were treated fairly or not. Robert E. Lee died in 1870, on September 28th. He had a stroke, then fell ill with pneumonia. He had become one of the most illustrious figures to stem out of the Civil War and was nothing short of a godly hero in the eyes of many.

On the 10th of May, the provisional president of the Confederacy, Jefferson Davis was captured. Andrew Johnson had issued a generous financial reward for whoever caught Davis and brought him to trial. His capture led to the birth of several misconceptions. The biggest one of them all, and the most humiliating for the ex-Confederate president, was the fact that, supposedly, he was caught as he attempted to flee dressed in women's clothing. According to his wife, he was not wearing any women's clothing, just a shawl to protect him against the cold. It did not really matter, as a surge of caricatures appeared in the newspapers of the day, featuring him dressed as a woman and attempting to flee from the Union soldiers.

He was taken to court (a quite odd aspect, given that Confederate soldiers were allowed to go unharmed and untried) and imprisoned in the Fortress Monroe on the 19th of May 1865. When Lincoln was shot, Davis was sad. While he was imprisoned, Pope Pius the 9th, himself imprisoned in the Vatican, is said to have sent him a crown of thorns, manually woven by himself, alongside a portrait. It is yet unclear if the crown was indeed woven by Pius or Davis's wife.

He spent two years in prison, then was released after many of his supporters posted a bail for him. They paid 100,000 dollars. After he was released, Jefferson Davis wrote the ultimate guide to the Confederacy - *The Rise and Fall of the Confederate Government* - that he published in 1881. Eight years later, he wrote another book: *A Short History of the Confederate States of America.*

Jefferson Davis died in 1889, on the 6th of December, after a long battle with bronchitis and malaria. He was buried in New Orleans, in Metairie Cemetery and afterward, at his wife's request, exhumed and re-interred in Richmond, in the Hollywood Cemetery. Even though he was the president of the Confederate States of America, he was hold in high regards after his death, as he had been a man of principle.

The four chaos-filled years of the Civil War had ended but, as we shall see next, this was far from being the end of the problems in the United States. It is safe to say that they only began. We will see why that is in the following chapters.

Misconceptions about the End of the Civil War

1. The Civil War came to an end at Appomattox

Formally, yes, the Civil War ended at Appomattox, when Lee surrendered to Grant, on the 19th of April, 1865. But informally, the battles lasted until the 23rd of June, when Stand Watie, who came to be known as the last Confederate general, surrendered his troops to Union general, Matthews.

2. The Union won because it had more money

The financial problems of the times were not confined to the borders of the South only. The North, too, had its fair share of trouble in this respect. When the war broke out, neither the South nor the North had the necessary funds. The Union did *not* win because it had a better economic stance. Far from it.

The Federal Income Tax was established in 1862 in the Union and one year later in the Confederacy.

3. No soldiers died at Palmito Ranch

No *Confederate* soldiers died at Palmito Ranch, the last battle of the Civil War. The Union lost between 4-30 privates. The last soldier who died in the Civil War was Union private John J. Williams.

Captivating Facts about the Period in Which the Civil War Was Ending

- Ulysses S. Grant had a tormenting migraine all throughout the Battle of Appomattox Court. It subsided when he got a letter from the Confederate Robert Lee, in which he expressed his desire to talk the terms of a surrender.
- After the Civil War ended, Robert E. Lee was not tried for treason. In fact, an insignificant number of Confederates were. However, he lost the right to vote as well as some of his property, which was transformed in a cemetery. He was a fervent supporter of civil rights for everybody but continued to oppose the right to vote of the African-Americans.
- Dysentery killed more soldiers in the Civil War than wounds. 95,000 soldiers, both from the Confederacy and the Union, lost their lives to this disease, whereas the number of those who perished because of their infected wounds was 83,700.
- The most famous song during the Civil War was "I wish I was in Dixie's Land." It was President Abraham Lincoln's favorite song, and he expressed his passion for it more than once. Daniel Decatur Emmett, the

writer of the song, reported: "If I had known to what use they were going to put my song, I will be damned if I'd have written it."

If the Choice Were Yours

- If you were Robert E. Lee, what would you have done? Would you have surrendered, like he did, or would you have ordered a retreat just to renew your forces and your strategies? Please remember that were it not for Lee's surrender to Grant, the Civil War would have lasted even longer.
- After Robert E. Lee surrendered, Ulysses Grant allowed the Confederate soldiers to go back to their homes unharmed and with no risk whatsoever of being tried and executed. If you were in his shoes, is this what you would have done, as well?
- If given a chance, would you imprison Jefferson Davis, or would you let him go his own way unharmed?

Chapter 6 - The Victory of the Union and the Results of the War

The Civil War lasted for four years, and even nowadays, researchers and historians alike have different opinions on what enabled the Union to be victorious over the Confederacy. Paradoxically, the last battle in the war, the one at Palmito Ranch ended with a Confederate victory.

The Civil War had begun with a small-scale conflict and so did it come to a halt, as if the four years of massacre didn't even take place. The Battle of Palmito Ranch gave birth to a lot of speculation on how the Confederates won it because they were numerically undermined (300 men) by the Union, who had 500 men. It has been speculated that they were helped by the French.

The literal end of the Civil War has been established to have been June 2nd, 1865. Edmund Kirby Smith, the Confederate general, surrendered both himself and his army to the Union on the 26th of May. This moment marks the dissolution of the Confederate army. Stand Watie followed in his footsteps. Andrew Johnson, the newly-appointed president after Abraham Lincoln's assassination, broke the blockade of the states in the South.

The total number of lives claimed during these four bloody years is yet debatable. For a long time, the supposed number of 650,000 was widely accepted, but opinions are divided. First of all, this definitely does not include civilian deaths. Second of all, it does not take into consideration all the immigrants that fought under the flag of the Union, as well as the freed African-American former slaves. The real, genuine number is unknown and will undoubtedly remain as such.

How Did the Union Win the War?

There are uncountable aspects that tip the scales in favor of the Union, even during the Civil War. On one hand, it had a lot more population than the Confederacy, although many of them did not want to fight against their Southern brothers. On the other hand, when you have a large number of people (approximately 22 million in the North), the industry is better.

Now, let's proceed to tactics. From the start, the Confederacy was in a defensive position, while the Union could not do anything else but charge in Confederate territory. This leads to heavy losses when a properly defended place is at play. Obviously, the number is God on the battlefield. No matter how much resistance an offensive army meets, the defensive one will always run out of fuel after a while.

One of the things that contributed to the downfall of the Confederacy is that the troops started to venture farther and farther into Union territory, thus leaving their defensive positions and doing the same thing the Union had done against them: lynch them while in defense.

Another factor that contributed to the victory of the Union is simple leadership. Jonathan Davis was a good politician and leader, but Abraham Lincoln was *born* to be a leader. It's a huge difference, although it does not look as such. In terms of military organization skills, Davis was not at all bad, and as proof stand the many defeats the Union has suffered at the hands of the Confederates.

With all these, Lincoln had a *huge* advantage: he created the Emancipation Proclamation. This gained him respect and overall likeability from the vast majority of the population, even from some Southerners. The eyes of the world, in this circumstance, were on the North, not on the South, and Davis could not match this... let's call it "approval rating." Of course, Lincoln did not live enough to see the post-war America, being assassinated by John Wilkes Booth on the 14th of April, 1865.

If you feel tempted to say that the Civil War was characterized by military genius, you should not. Many of the generals and the soldiers who fought during this conflict were painfully inexperienced. There really was no "tactics" better than the others. It was just bloodshed from the start to the end.

Military leadership played a crucial role in ensuring the victory of the Union, as well. Historians agreed that while the Confederate generals were not incompetent, Davies usually listened to bad advice. For instance, for the whole extent of the war, the Confederate tactics implied attacking then retreating and defending whatever there was to defend instead of pushing forwards and seizing the numerous opportunities they had.

This was a major mistake because it allowed the forces of the Union to slaughter these retreating troops and to siege all the places they used as a shelter. It is true, on the other hand, that the Union was incredibly crippled by the Confederacy more than once. That, however, was just the course of the war.

The Results

The Civil War was cataclysmic for the United States of America, and it applied to demographics, finances, industry and pretty much all levels of society. The financial cost of these four years of pandemonium has been estimated to well over $6 billion, and this sum is only for the North.

Millions of dollars were spent on a daily basis (yes, that's correct, *daily*). The Confederacy spent less, around $2 billion, but it is perfectly understandable, given that it did not have a booming industry, like the North. The costs were further heightened by the complete devastation left behind both in the South and the North. Crops had been burned to the ground, homes leveled and farms pillaged.

This destruction was almost entirely found in the South. As one might expect, the debt of the USA also grew. When the war ended in 1865, the national debt was very close to $3 billion. Notwithstanding, there is a positive outcome out of this pool of negativity: the Civil War contributed a great deal to America becoming a leading industrial power. When it comes to demographics, it has been claimed that over 1 million people lost their lives during the Civil War (so not 650,000).

The South was relying heavily on its cotton export, but once the Anaconda Plan went into effect, it suffered an unprecedented inflation. Moreover, it also relied on slave labor. When Lincoln launched the Emancipation Proclamation, the South took an unexpected – and as heavy as unexpected – fall. The main two things the South counted on the most were immediately taken out of its reach, leaving it like a deer caught in the headlights of a truck.

Meanwhile, the North was thriving. This was evidently a decisive factor in its victory over the South, primarily because the Union produced so much more weapons and iron. The Confederacy could never compete with its enemy in this respect. Economy, too, was increasingly better in the North than it was in the South. The economic factor was vital in the Civil War and not only – due to its good economy, the North was able to keep this trend going even after the war.

The African-American population was extremely happy that the Civil War eventually drew to an end, but the protection they had hoped for vanished with Abraham Lincoln. Even though the Emancipation Proclamation clearly stipulated they were free, the death of the president left them uncovered.

Many persons strove to bring slavery back or at least become dominant again.

Unfortunately, it is now that radical white supremacy groups like the infamous Ku Klux Klan appeared. The war was over, indeed, but it was just the beginning for tons of other problems. The Constitution also suffered some modifications in the post-war period, by having three new amendments added to it: the 13th, 14th and 15th.

These were direct products of war since all three tackle the same issue: equality of races and no slave ownership. The 13th states that slavery is inconceivable; the 14th states that all people born in the United States have American citizenship and lastly, the 15th gave all people the right to vote, regardless of race. The America of the 21st century, the great melting pot of today, could not have been possible without the implementation of these three amendments.

The post-war period saw numerous other changes that affected nearly all levels of American society. Paper currency (national), for instance, is one of those things made possible by the Civil War. The state-of-the-art medical system was implemented during the Civil War, as well, when people started to become more versed in biology and human anatomy to serve on the front.

Even the two political sides that exist today on American soil, the Democrats and the Republicans are remnants of this 4-year carnage. One could go on for a while about the results of the Civil War. In the following chapter, we will see how reconstruction went, especially for the ruined South, as well as delve deeper in how exactly this conflict shaped the America we see today. But first, let's settle a bit on Lincoln's assassination.

The First American Presidential Assassination

On the 14th of April, 1865, Abraham Lincoln was at Ford's Theatre, watching a play. John Wilkes Booth was a quite famous actor, but he had a well-hidden secret. He worked as a spy for the Confederacy. He never had a taste for Lincoln, and this barely degenerated when the president offered the African American population its metaphorical freedom.

Lincoln was shot in the back of the head and point-blank, having no chance for survival at such a short distance. He went into a coma for 9 hours. A surgeon tried to clear his wound of the blood clot that had formed there, but the wound itself was too deep for the president to have any chance of surviving. Booth was caught 12 days later and killed. What is interesting about the assassination is the sorrow it produced among the African American communities. The United States had lost their president, but the disadvantaged African Americans had lost the only person that at least made an attempt to give them their freedom.

Lincoln's funeral procession extended from Washington D.C. to Illinois, in Springfield. Huge masses of people attended the memorials that took place in all the cities the procession passed through.

Abraham Lincoln went down in history as one of the greatest presidents of the country and is honored to this day as an excellent leader and a liberator of the African American population. Andrew Johnson, who took the leadership after Lincoln's death, attempted to follow his footsteps, but his plans backfired more often than not due to poor political skills.

Misconceptions about the Post-War Period

1. The Civil War claimed the highest number of American lives in the history of the country

This seems to be everyone's opinion; there is no denying that. However, it is far from being true. Yes, the Civil War was an incredibly bloody war, but more American soldiers were killed in the Second World War, and that's a fact. Most of the soldiers that fought in the Civil War died of disease, not in combat, so they do not really qualify as casualties recorded in action, on the battlefield.

2. The Confederacy lost because it didn't want to win

Yes, it sounds surreal, but it's actually a historical opinion that belongs to E. Merton Coulter, an American historian. He opines that the Confederate soldiers were eventually crushed by the Union because they didn't want to win as badly as the ones of the Union did. As one might expect, this is not the case. We are pretty sure that no Confederate soldier went on the battlefield bored out of his wits. Shelby Foote, another historian, opined that the South never stood a chance anyway.

3. The last words Abraham Lincoln heard were: "You sockdologizing old man-trap"

Those are said to have been part of a play. We are quite sure that there is absolutely no way to tell what a man who has been shot in the head heard for the last time. This is a misconception by excellence. Therefore, it needs to be debunked. Unfortunately, we cannot find out what the last words he heard were, and if we did, it would probably make no difference whatsoever.

Fascinating Facts about the Post-War Period

- According to a conspiracy theory, John Wilkes Booth was not killed at the Garrett Farm, but fled instead and died a few years later by his own hands.
- The African American population was broken-hearted when President Abraham Lincoln was assassinated.
- Walt Whitman, the transcendentalist poet, wrote four poems about Abraham Lincoln and his passing. The most famous of all of them is *When Lilacs Last in the Dooryard Bloom'd*.

If the Choice Were Yours

- Let's imagine for a moment that you are John Wilkes Booth. Would you press the trigger of the gun whose echo would resound through the ages, killing one of the greatest men that America has ever given to the world?
- The South was extremely disadvantaged by the North's booming industry and economy, both of them being decisive factors in the loss of the former. If you were in charge, is there something you could have done to bring the South on the right track, economy and industry-wise? Do you think anything at all could have been changed to tip the scales in favor of the Confederacy, at least a tiny bit or not?

Chapter 7 - The Reconstruction and How the War Shaped America

As mentioned before, the Civil War had left the South in ruins. Reconstruction, therefore, was easier said than done. The economy had been built on slave ownership, but now they were freed. The dollar of the South was worthless. Also, farming became one of the most widespread jobs. The slave owners, once aristocratic entities, had been reduced to the status of simple workers. Don't make any mistakes however – this didn't happen overnight.

Plans for reconstruction were there even before the Civil War ended. For instance, in 1863, Lincoln launched the Proclamation of Amnesty and Reconstruction, also known as the 10 percent plan. However, this was more of a scheme for restoring peace between the Union and the Confederacy than reconstructing America. When Lincoln was assassinated, Andrew Johnson came to power.

Andrew Johnson was the first president in the history of the US to be impeached, due to his clashes with the Congress. His Democratic Party and the Republican Party got in numerous conflicts over the years he was in office. During the elections in 1866, Johnson lost much of his political prowess in favor of the Republicans. First of all, he was in favor of white supremacy, as he tried to undermine the African-American population and its rights on multiple occasions. Second of all, he had what has come to be known as "delusions of grandeur."

In an instance from 1866, during a speech in support of his political campaign, he likened himself to Jesus Christ. It was obvious for pretty much everyone that he was not actually fit to be president since he was obsessed with himself. Accordingly, nowadays (and back in the day, obviously) he is seen as one of the worst presidents the United States of America ever had.

His reconstruction plans were a lot more radical than Lincoln's. Apparently, he was more in favor of the South than the North, and that aspect upset a lot of people. Most Southerners regained their properties and were pardoned for their deeds against the North. Needless to say, many people thought that Southerners had to be punished, not pardoned. This was somewhat a paradoxical action from Johnson's part because he was extremely eager to have Jefferson Davis, the former president of the Confederacy tried and punished.

The Reconstruction also saw the rise of a new political power: the Republican Party. This was formed by now emancipated African Americans and white abolitionists. If we think about it for a minute there, this marks the moment when democracy in America truly deserves its name, because it mingles the two most prevalent races in the country and they now have equal rights. African Americans had the freedom to vote and were seen as American citizens.

With all these, in 1865 and 1866, the so-called "black codes" started to appear. These were meant to restore the power of the white people in the former Confederacy, as well as re-establish their power *over* the African Americans. How could this happen when Lincoln clearly stated that the slaves had been freed? It's simple: Johnson gave the South the liberty to form its own governments. Obviously, that was a huge mistake.

It was a sign that the Civil War had been fought for precisely nothing, since nothing much changed. These Black Codes were disastrous for the African-American population. They were not allowed to get an education, be it as simple as learning how to write and read, they were not authorized to walk in public spaces, they had no right whatsoever to own or buy any piece of land, etc. Moreover, some states in the South introduced "convict leasing," which was the same old slavery, but under a new appearance.

Under "convict leasing," the African-Americans who got arrested had to work on plantations or to harvest wood for certain individuals. The North, as you might expect, was going insane over these black codes. Again, it was further proof that hundreds of thousands of people had lost their lives for nothing. If one of the reasons why the Civil War had occurred was indeed the emancipation of the African-Americans, then it was a gratuitous bloodshed. White supremacy was clearer and sterner than it had ever been, even before the war started.

The Jim Crow laws, which started to be promulgated in 1896, further deepened the racial chasm between whites and African-Americans. These laws called for segregation in all social respects. Therefore, the African-Americans and the whites had to be separated. Schools were to be segregated, housing, too, jobs, everything. Even the very name of the laws were discriminatory, because "Jim Crow" was a term for "negro." Unfortunately, these laws took decades to be removed. It will be in 1964, when the Civil Rights Act appeared, that all the damage would be mended, albeit partially.

Once again, the North had a bone to pick with the South, and it will be only under the Radical Reconstruction that these codes would be once again rendered inefficient. The Freedman's Bureau was formed as a means to provide some help to the African American population. Under the Radical Reconstruction, most states in the former Confederacy were returned to the Union. The Republican Party had an influence on them all.

Things took a turn for the better once Johnson was impeached and Ulysses S. Grant became the 18th president of the United

States of America. The newly-appointed president was a lot more open to change than his predecessor. He advocated equal rights for everybody and strove to make the Americans look upon the Native Americans with respect and eventually learn from their culture. The discrimination against the African Americans also started to subside during the years in which Grant was the president.

The KKK, who terrorized black neighborhoods and persecuted all African Americans in the south, were arrested after Grant issued the Enforcement Acts. The Klan did not have much power after Grant became president. Helped by Amos T. Akerman, his Attorney General, he started to persecute the members who were caught by the federal troops.

The KKK

The African American people became increasingly freer after the end of the Civil War, but things were far from being resolved. The South was very much against their emancipation and the fact that they seemed to be more favored at the time than the whites. This lead to the formation of violent groups that dealt damage to the black community. The most known of them all is the Ku Klux Klan, KKK. The KKK worked in two stages, with the most recent one going on since 1915. The first one was formed as fast as the Civil War ended and lasted until 1880.

The KKK was the irrefutable proof that most veterans of the Confederacy were not willing to say farewell to arms yet. For them, it was inconceivable that the African American population was given equal rights with their white peers. This led to a chain of crimes against the black community and to years of terror. Of course, the KKK was not the only organization, but it was the most powerful. In just a couple of years, it reached millions of members.

Soon enough, it borrowed certain ideas from Nazism, and all members sported the swastika. Hitler had become an icon within the KKK because he would not have allowed a minority to have equal rights with the native (ironically, not native) population, as proved during the Holocaust. When activists were asking for the quicker implementation of the equal civil rights, the KKK often organized large-scale suppressions against them, using violence to quench them down.

There are three known "waves" of the Ku Klux Klan: one came immediately after the Civil War and lasted until 1871; the second activated between 1914 and 1944 and the third one started in 1946 and still activates to this day, although not as overtly as it used to in the past.

The Racial Problem During the Reformation

The Reformation is usually seen as a highly beneficial and innovative period in the history of the United States. However, it also has its downsides. During this time, the "distinction" between the races became so much clearer than it already was during the Civil War and before it.

This accounts for the huge variety of hate crimes that took place during this period. Eventually, the African Americans gained equal privileges, although those came at a very high price. One of the reasons why blacks were still – or even more – persecuted was that the new president, Andrew Johnson, was quite racist. That is no secret. He made his opinions vis-à-vis the African American people public more than once, and all of them were met with fierce critique. Johnson became, at some point, a racist clown.

Many historians accuse him of being too inflexible to make real changes in the context of the Reformation because he failed to see it for the incredible Revolution it was. Traces of the anti-African American groups that formed during this time can be seen in the United States of today, since the KKK is very much alive, unfortunately.

Racial segregation, as it was called, became widespread. This vouched for the African American population to be restricted to living in designated areas (which can be seen today, too). This did not happen only in the United States, of course. Segregation can be seen in the history of most countries in the world, even though it might not be targeted against the African American communities.

It is only that in the United States, it was so much more evident, especially after the Civil War ended, but not necessarily restricted to that period.

The American Civil Rights Movement

Although this happened during the 20th century, long after the Civil War, it is this conflict in question that gave the start to it. Why do we mention it? Because it supports our argument that race became an incredibly obvious problem in the postwar period. Even though the African Americans were now free and with relatively the same rights as the whites, they were still highly underprivileged.

The rights that had come with the new three amendments were superficial. In truth, in order to be in effect, a right has to be secured by the state. It goes without saying that this was not the case.

The movements started in 1954 and ended in 1968 and sought to stop racial segregation once and for all. The fact that there was a need for these actions to take place stands to show how embedded discrimination was in everyday America, and how long it took to render the Jim Crow laws and the Black Codes inefficient. It is sad but simultaneously true. Even after the Civil Rights Act from 1964, another two years of protests were needed for equal rights.

How the War Shaped America

The Civil War shook the United States of America to the core. It influenced modern society in approximately any way a conflict could impact future generations. Let's see some of the most known things this war introduced to nowadays America.

The most important aspects to stem out of the 4-year Civil War and to have the greatest influence on the United States of the 21st century were the three amendments. Of course, if we go a little back and we re-read the information, we can clearly see these were much of a fiasco, for years to come since they were introduced.

Moreover, after the Civil War ended, the South came in line with the North and America became a single nation. Obviously, it took decades until Southerners accepted that they had no other direction in which to go but the one that led to compliance with their Northern brothers. The "one single nation under God" would not have been possible were it not for the Civil War.

This war also influenced the American society in terms of medicine. It was certainly not pleasant at all to have been wounded during that time since medicine was very rudimentary. However, that led to an increasingly better system.

As we've seen, most people give in to believing that many soldiers preferred to shoot themselves in the head than to fall into the hands of the surgeons, who apparently had a penchant for amputations. This is not true. They used chloroform to anesthetize the wounded soldiers, and only afterward performed severing the limbs that ought to be severed.

Unfortunately, a lot of mercury was used during the Civil War as medicine. It was called "blue mass" and it was a concoction of mercury, licorice and rose honey, among others. Mercury is highly poisonous, but this was not known at the time. Even President Abraham Lincoln was prescribed Blue Mass for his frequent bouts of melancholy. The use of this "medicine" obviously led to mercury poisoning. It was later on banned. Researchers made a few attempts at finding out whether Lincoln was suffering from mercury poisoning, but they could not get any conclusive results since they could not procure hair.

The fact that nowadays we have ambulances can be retraced back to the Civil War, but not many people seem to know that. Jonathan Letterman, a surgeon that lived and served during the war, is the one we have to thank for having hospitals and ambulances.

In those days, of course, ambulances existed in an inchoate form, as they were wagons in which the wounded were put and carried as quickly as possible to the first aid tents. Rudimentary or not, these "ambulances" saved a lot of lives during the war and served as a prototype for the ones we have today. Letterman used to create movable hospitals (medical tents, really) where he admitted and treated the wounded soldiers. He invented the concept of triage and used it probably for the first time in history. Today, we know it as "priority."

Those in need of immediate medical care were admitted first; those with superficial wounds always followed after them. Neurology, too, is an inheritance from the Civil War. The first neurology hospital was formed in Philadelphia in 1861, by three doctors: Silas Weir Mitchell, William Keen, and George Morehouse. The trio is credited with introducing the medical world to several neurological diseases, including the phantom limb condition.

The national income tax, as well, was introduced after the war ended, in an effort to muster the money to pay for the expenses. Technology saw a tremendous explosion during the 19th century, which established the United States of America as one of the leading countries regarding technological output. If the Civil War had not taken place, America would not have been an industrialized country today, and that's a fact.

Both sides, the South and the North, were in a fierce competition in regards with industrialization. Obviously, the North was leading, but once they were united, ideas started to merge. It is quite easy to understand why this was so *extremely* important for the history of America.

The South and the North developed at their own pace; certain ideas developed in the North, but did not evolve in the South and vice-versa. When the Civil War came to an end, and the two came together as a whole, these ideas came together as well, creating brand-new notions that served the American society ever since.

Prior to this, America was basically formed from two countries. Two nations mean two economies, therefore division on all the levels of society. Once the war ended, and the Confederacy slowly disappeared, this division was repaired, as well, making the United States, for the first time in history, one single nation. Everything else is just related to this aspect.

In order to understand how millions of people were willing to commit to a bloody war for four years, we have to be aware of the fact that both sides were fighting for *ideals*. When this happens, the conflict is never easy and short-lived. Fortunately, the civil war proved both the South and the North that things could be solved with diplomacy rather than by clubbing each other to death.

And this is precisely the greatest inheritance of the Civil War: it showed the people that they were indeed one nation, in spite of the fact that "Southerners" and "Northerners" were still in circulation. The same terms are used even today, often with a pejorative sense attached to them.

The Most Frequent Misconceptions about the Reconstruction and Post-Reconstruction America

1. The African-American population was not enslaved anymore

Terribly wrong. We've seen that in the decades after the Civil War, the African-American population was even more discriminated than in the period prior to the war. Slavery was abolished, that's right, but under the Black Codes, for instance, the African-Americans led a more impoverished and miserable life than they used to. Under the Jim Crow laws, again, they suffered more than they suffered when they were enslaved. Slavery was just not a physical act anymore after the Reconstruction, but it was a mental one.

2. Andrew Johnson was not a racist

Unfortunately, he was. In fact, he was one of the biggest racists that ever lived on American soil. In a speech he delivered in Indianapolis, he said: "I have lived among Negroes, all my life, and I am for this Government with slavery under the Constitution as it is. I am for the Government of my fathers with Negroes, I am for it without Negroes. Before I would see this Government destroyed, I would send every negro back to Africa, disintegrated and blotted out of space." (source: <u>Real Life Villains</u>) If you need some other proof that he was a racist, then you have the liberty to research his life.

3. The KKK only targeted African-Americans

No. While it is true that the favorite target of the organization was represented by the African-Americans, they sought to crush under their feet all minorities from the US, including Jews, especially after their ideology was seeped in Hitler's Nazism. Moreover, they were against *all* immigrants, regardless of nationality, color of skin or religious beliefs. Fortunately enough, we are not bothered by the KKK today, as it got fewer and fewer followers by the year.

Some Interesting Facts about America During and After the Reconstruction

- All over the world, the abolishment of slavery was done naturally. The US is the only country where slavery had to be abolished through bloodshed. So much for the all-tolerant melting pot, isn't it? If slavery would have been abolished peacefully, the Civil War would not have taken place, saving, in the process, the lives of almost one million Americans who died in battle and/or ridden with disease.
- In the 19th century, the Bible was the best-selling book; the second one was *Uncle Tom's Cabin*, by Harriet Beecher Stowe. It was published in 1855 and quickly became one of the most famous books not only in America but in the entire world. It sold millions of copies and is still re-issued year after year.

- Hiram Rhodes Revels was the first African American to become a Senator in the U.S. Congress. The first African American president of the United States was Barrack Obama, in office from 2009 to 2017.
- There are many theories concerning the etymology of "Ku Klux Klan." The most widespread one is that "Ku Klux Klan" is the sound produced by cocking a shotgun. This is also the most probable one. The explanation comes from a Sherlock Holmes novel, written by Sir Arthur Conan Doyle, who lived when the KKK activated for the first time. There are several others. For instance, some think it comes from the Greek word "kuklos" (circle), but no further proof is given and at this stage, it does not make any sense whatsoever.

Conclusion

America's history is unique in the world. Although it is not as ancient as the history of a European country, it is replete with events that changed the entire world. We all know it as a "melting pot," a place where all kinds of nationalities and races find solace and live with each other in harmony. Even to this day, America holds its status of "promised land" for a lot of people all over the world who, very much like the settlers of yore, go there to find their freedom.

Of course, none of these could have been possible without the Civil War. It might sound unethical, but sometimes war is necessary for a country to progress. If there is no conflict, this will eventually translate into "no progress," just stagnation. One of the most important things related to the Civil War is that, for the first time in American history, the African American population was given a voice. This will give birth to an entire array of movements in pursuit of full freedom and equality between races.

We must not forget that the Civil War is the main reason why the United Stated today is a single country, not two separate ones that live by each other. Celebrating the 4th of July, for example, is also a remnant of the Civil War. There was no other conflict in the history of the US to affect its future on such a scale as this one, and there will probably be no other.

We've learned pretty much everything one needs to learn about the Civil War in this book. We've seen what led to it and what the political environment was like at the time. We explained how it all began, how it unfolded and the fronts it was fought on. We also presented the most important battles in its context, the battles fought on water, the various tactics employed by both sides and most importantly, how these four years affected the birth of an entirely new nation.

For Europeans, the history of the USA is as fascinating as the history of Europe is for Americans. That is by no means trivial. People learn from each other, usually from each other's mistakes. Different objectives often lead to conflict, but that is just one of the aspects of life we are all faced with at some point or another.

I hope you have found this book useful. There is a lot of information on the Internet, but it is either biased or inaccurate. When studying history, bias and inaccuracy are the greatest problems. Sources can be completely made up, so that would not be much of a history, but more of a fictional work. By reading this book, you will assimilate accurate information based on facts.

Finally, you can recommend it to some of your friends who might have an interest in studying the Civil War but found no simple presentation on it as of now. Learn from history, because you are among those who must make sure it doesn't repeat itself.

20596321R00045

Printed in Poland
by Amazon Fulfillment
Poland Sp. z o.o., Wrocław